TEENS SPEAK
BOYS AGES 13 to 15

Sixty Original
Character Monologues

by Kristen Dabrowski

KIDS SPEAK SERIES

A Smith and Kraus Book

A Smith and Kraus Book
Published by Smith and Kraus, Inc.
177 Lyme Road, Hanover, NH 03755
www.smithkraus.com

First Edition: March 2005
Manufactured in the United States of America
10 9 8 7 6 5 4 3 2 1

Cover and text design by Julia Gignoux, Freedom Hill Design
Library of Congress Cataloging-in-Publication
Dabrowski, Kristen.
Boys speak, ages 13–15 ; sixty character monologues / by Kristen Dabrowski.
—1st ed.
p. cm. — (Kids speak series)
ISBN 1-57525-413-1
1. Monologues—Juvenile literature. 2. Acting—Juvenile literature. I. Title: Boys
speak, ages thirteen to fifteen. II. Title: Boys speak, ages thirteen through fifteen.
III. Title. IV. Series.

PN2080.D333 2005
812'.6—dc22
2004059047

CONTENTS

For Bob and Julie

Foreword

Hello, actors! Inside this book, you'll find sixty monologues for boys aged 13 to 15.

Here's how they are organized:

- There are six sections in the book. Each section includes ten monologues from the point of view of one character. Each character is described on his own introduction page.

- Each character was designed to have different experiences and views on the world. You'll see him in school, at home, with strangers, etc.

How to choose a monologue:

- You may want to begin by looking at the character descriptions. Choose a character most like you, or for a challenge, choose one that is quite different from yourself.

- Page through the monologues. There are dramatic, comic, and semicomic monologues in each section. Some characters are more comic or dramatic than others.

- Trust your instincts!

How to perform the monologues:

- Tell your story clearly.

- Know to whom you're speaking and imagine you are talking to just that one person. (Of course, if you're talking to more people, keep that in mind as well!)

- A new paragraph or *(Beat.)* means that there is a pause due to a subject change or another (imaginary) person speaking. Be sure that you know what the unseen person is saying.

- Play around with the monologue and try doing it a lot of different ways.

Have fun!

Kristen Dabrowski

CLAY HALBURTON

Clay is shy, studious, and a little bit neurotic. He has a lot of inner strength and determination. His parents are university professors and he is an only child.

SPLITTING HAIRS

Clay, comic
At the barbershop, talking to the barber.

In what universe did you think this would be a good idea? Look at what you did to me. Oh my God, I can't go to school. I can't go anywhere. Don't tell me to calm down. Listen, this may come as a shock to you, but school is not an easy place. It's a literal nightmare, if you must know. Worse than anything you can imagine. And FYI, it's especially bad for me. I'm smart, mister. This is the kiss of death for a kid. Not only that, but my parents are smart, too. They, like, live a life of the mind. You'd think that maybe because they're university professors or something that they'd maybe have more of a clue about what the younger generation was into, but they don't. Hence the five dollar haircut you just gave me. To them, how you look isn't important. If I had a dollar for every speech that started, "It's the inside that counts . . ." I'd have, like, twenty billion dollars. But they are completely wrong, of course, in this instance.

You basically just hung a sign on my back that says, "Kick me, repeatedly." Thanks a lot. Are you a sadist or something? Do you think this is funny?

Well, see you next time. If I live long enough for my hair to grow.

WELCOME TO GEEKDOM, POPULATION: YOU

Clay, semicomic
At home, talking to his mother.

You realize this is completely hypocritical. I can't even believe you're saying it. I can't believe you have the guts . . . *I* need to be more social and interact more with people my age? What about you? What about you? You and Dad never do anything. You don't have any friends. You only have colleagues, coworkers. You are—it is *rich* for you to be lecturing me on socializing. You don't even know the meaning of the word. *(Beat.)* Fine. Whatever. So you know the *meaning* of the word, but you don't know how to do it yourself. You're not exactly a role model here.

You can't just *force* me to suddenly be a popular, sociable guy. *(Beat.)* That *is* what you're saying. Go out there and be popular. I'm not popular. I never will be. I have no idea how to be popular. It's like I don't speak the language. It's like being foreign. I don't even understand it. You can't force these things to happen. It's like a gift you're born with or not. And I'm not. And it's your fault. Because you're my mother. And Dad's my father. I didn't have a chance. I'm born into geekdom. I'm doomed to geekdom. And you can't change that just because you suddenly want a cool kid. It doesn't work like that. I thought you'd be smart enough to know that.

THE WORLD OF TOMORROW

Clay, comic
At school, talking to a girl.

Do you want to come over and work on the assignment? I could help you out with it. It's not my best subject, but I'm not bad either. I could probably help you get an A, or at least a B. We could hang out, too. My parents will probably let us get a pizza. And they wouldn't bother us much. We'd be mostly alone.

I don't know if you know this, Sasha, but I'm basically guaranteed to be rich someday. Honestly. I'm not saying that to be a jerk or something. It's true. I'm going to start my own major technology company. Like Bill Gates, but with a better haircut. Either that or be a movie director like Quentin Tarantino. I bet you'd be great in the movies, like an actress or something. That is, if you want that sort of thing.

So, anyhow, what do you think? Want to come over to my house tonight? It doesn't even have to be for a long time or anything. I could help you, I think. If you wanted help. And it would be fun, maybe. What do you say? Not that you have to. It's just an idea.

AWKWARD

Clay, dramatic
At home, talking to his mother.

Mom, how do you know if you've gone mentally insane? Because I think I have. Or I will. I cannot sleep, ever. I haven't slept for days and I don't think I can take it anymore.

I don't know why. I'm just, like, stressed. About everything! *(Beat.)* Listen, I don't think I can talk to you about this. I don't know. It's just not appropriate. It's just that . . . God, I'm a loser. I should have, I don't know, friends to talk to or something. It's just that . . . Promise you won't make a big deal out of this. It's just that . . . I like this girl. Don't, Mom! Don't! Don't make any "that's so cute" noises or I will hate you forever. I mean it. Because, if you must know, she hates me. She does. She's not playing hard to get or being shy, she hates me. And, I don't know, I just like her. It's, like, chemical or something. I can't help it. So, I don't know what to do. Is there some sort of way to flush this out of my system? Because I feel sick all the time. Sick. I'm a loser and everything's, like, terrible. Never mind. I should never have said anything. Forget I said anything. Please, Mom, pretend this conversation never happened. I hate my life, I swear. I'm a freak of nature.

UNSPEAKABLE

Clay, semicomic
At school, talking to a girl.

Listen, do you have to dress like that? Of course you can dress however you want, but . . . Did you ever consider that people might not want to see your, like, underwear? *(Beat.)* Don't be dense. You know what I mean. Your . . . panties or whatever. I don't get this thing. Where your pants are really low and your . . . underthings are really . . . exposed. Maybe people don't actually need to see that. Maybe it's under your clothes for a reason. It's called *under*wear, after all.

I wasn't *looking*. It's not like you can miss it. They are bright pink, after all. Don't be so vain. It's not like everyone is looking at you all the time. And I'm certainly not looking. It's just in my eye line. Or it was. When I was sitting and you were standing in front of me. It's like you were daring me to look. But I wasn't *looking*.

Listen, anyhow, exactly what message are you sending to people when you show your underthings like that? *(Beat.)* I'm not saying anything, I'm just saying think about it. It does make you seem a little slutty. *(Beat.)* I'm not saying anything! Take it easy! Keep your pants on! *(Beat.)* That's an *expression*. Jeez, read a book, maybe!

FEEL THE BURN

Clay, comic
At a doctor's office, talking to the doctor.

I'm fine, actually. As usual, my mom is just freaking out.

Well, the problem is . . . It's just that . . . I can't sleep. And I'm depressed. And I'm a loser. And no one likes me. And my stomach is burning. I double over in pain. I feel like I'm going to puke. And I can't run. And I seem to have no muscles or anything. I know I must because I'm not, like, unable to move or anything, but I'm really weak. And I get tired a lot. And I get these massive headaches. My head pounds and pounds like I have this vein that's trying to pump all my blood into my head at once. It's like a really big drum that keeps banging and banging. I taste acid in my mouth all the time. So I worry that I have bad breath. I eat a lot of mints. I'm just, like, tired. Sick and tired. But I'm OK. I mean, I'll live. It's not like I'm dying or anything. I'm just sick to my stomach all the time. But it's no big deal.

So . . . I'll just be going now. OK? I think I need to puke anyway.

SITTING DOWN

Clay, dramatic
At school, talking to a few classmates.

Um, what are you doing to Dave? *(Beat.)* It looks like you're about to kick his butt. *(Beat.)* Well, how come? *(Beat.)* "Because" isn't a very good reason and he's, like, my friend. Could you maybe not kick his butt? Maybe? Isn't there, like, something else you could do instead?

(Backing up.) No, kicking *my* butt isn't really what I had in mind. At all. I meant something completely different. *(Beat.)* I don't know what! I'm just . . . I just . . . Listen, could you just . . . I really have to . . . I'm not sure it would be wise. Did you ever think maybe you could get in trouble for this?

Come to think of it, I'm sorry to interrupt. Why don't you go on with what you were doing. I have to get to class anyhow and . . . Sorry! Sorry, I . . . gotta go!

MATURE

Clay, comic
At school, talking to a friend.

She's not that bad. I'm just saying you can't tell everything by how someone dresses. She's actually pretty smart, actually. You wouldn't actually think so, but . . . *(Beat.)* I do not like her! Please. As if I would. She's not exactly my type.

What is my type? I don't know. I'm a kid still, I'm working it out. But I know she's not it. *(Beat.)* Do you really think she's . . . slutty? I don't think so. I really don't. I think she just doesn't think about her . . . impact. With clothes and stuff. I mean, she talks to me and is even sometimes nice about it. Let's face it, most girls won't be decent and normal at all. At least not to me. And sometimes she is. Sometimes she's not, but . . . I think she's nice, that's all. And not totally uninteresting and unintelligent.

I don't like her! Maybe *you* like her!

TERRIFYING

Clay, comic
At home, talking to a girl.

So, it's good you came over. I mean, so we can do homework. That's all. Not like I like you or anything. *(Beat.)* No, you're not unattractive, I'm just saying . . . I mean, I thought you'd want to know that I'm not, like, being all . . . you know. Maybe we should start working.

Are you OK? I mean, are you crying? Because you could maybe tell me what's bothering you. If you want. But if you're OK, maybe we should get to work. But if you're upset like your life is ruined, you could tell me. *(Beat.)* Listen, I can kind of tell you're upset—

I didn't mean anything! I mean, I think you're kind of great. Kind of. A little. I mean, all I meant was you're not ugly, but I'm not trying to jump your bones or anything. So . . . so . . . about this project . . .

But we were just getting started! Can we get together later then? When you're not . . . Bye, then!

THE STAND

Clay, dramatic
At home, talking to his parents.

Look, did you ever think that maybe you shouldn't butt in? Because you don't know everything? Because you don't. Know everything. She's nice. I like her. And she . . . she actually likes me, too, I think. Maybe this is something that didn't occur to you, but it is possible for a girl to like me. I am, after all, a guy. And I'm not a little kid. You can't tell me what to do. If I want to go out with her, I will. It's not a big deal. *(Beat.)* I'm not too young! I swear, you live in the Dark Ages. I have a chance not to be a loser geek here and I'd really like to take it.

Stop it! Don't judge her. She's not . . . a person is not what they wear. They're who they are from the inside. You say that crap all the time. Now's your chance to show you mean it. Sasha is pretty and smart and nice and I like her. I'm not saying we're going to get married or anything, for Chrissake, we're kids, but . . . I'm going to hang out with her. I am.

It's none of your business what we do. But . . . nothing, OK? So let's shut up about it already. It's embarrassing! She probably will reject me anyway, so it doesn't even matter.

MATT SANDERS

Impulsive, talkative, and outgoing, Matt has a lot of friends and a few enemies due to his big mouth. He lives with his father, his stepmother, and three of his sisters.

SICK

Matt, semicomic
At home, talking to his father.

Um, she's a girl. I know it's hard to tell, but I'm pretty sure about this one, seeing as her name is Tina.

I can't share my room with a girl! *(Beat.)* I *know* she's my sister, duh, but that actually almost makes it worse, not better! I'm too old to share a room with my sister. It's kind of perverted and sick. I mean, where am I supposed to change my clothes? It's hard enough getting privacy in this house.

It doesn't matter that it's only for a short time. And it's not a short time—her entire winter break for college—it's a long time! Why can't she share with Angela, Laura, and Marnie? *(Beat.)* There is too enough room.

I know this is going to make you mad, but also she's not even my sister. She's my *half*-sister. She's practically a stranger and she's old and she's a *girl*.

What if I camp out in the backyard? What about that? That would be better. At least it wouldn't be perverted.

GIRL TALK

Matt, semicomic
At school, talking to his friends.

Unfortunately, I know a little bit about this, with my sisters and all. Not a lot, that would be disgusting. But they don't talk about stuff like on TV. Like maxi pads. I swear, I'd vomit if they did.

The stuff girls talk about is way more boring, actually. They talk about clothes and TV and stuff. They don't talk about the same shows as us, of course. They watch all kinds of stupid shows where people get makeovers to look uglier than before. They make these old women wear clothes that are too tight and all stretched across their fat stomachs on these shows, I swear. It's hysterical. And they watch these stupid house shows where people make rooms really, really ugly. Like no normal person would ever live in these houses. The walls are always painted, like, pink. And the people on these shows are so completely cheerful it's wrong. It should be against the law. And then they have all these boring conversations about should they have done the stencil on the wall and stuff. *(Beat.)* A stencil is when they draw ugly patterns on the wall or something.

I do not watch these shows! But it's not like I have a choice sometimes. I'm trapped!

FRIENDSHIP

Matt, semicomic
At home, talking to his best friend.

You can't leave. I'm serious. This is critical. The minute you walk out that door, my stepmom will yell at me. *(Beat.)* Because we ate all the stuff in the fridge! She's nuts about that. I'm supposed to ask before I do anything. It's nuts. I never used to have to do that. It's my house, too, right? But she's really concerned about everything being in *exactly* the right place. The other day I put my coat down on the sofa and she was all, "Matt! Come and pick your coat up now! You have no manners!" And she kept going on and on like that. And I left it there for, like, five minutes. My mom would have just thrown it in the closet or left it or at least asked nicely. She's a bitch. I don't know why my dad likes her. She's obsessed with organization. How could anyone be obsessed with organization? Is there anything duller in the universe? She wants me to be a robot or something. News flash—I'm human.

I think she just hates guys. She hates you, too. *(Beat.)* Well, you're my alibi, that's why. When my coat is on the sofa, I tell her you did it. When there's no food in the fridge, I say you did it. *(Beat.)* It's a matter of survival, so get used to it, moron.

CAUGHT

Matt, dramatic
At home, talking to his father.

Dad, who was . . . ? Dad, I know. I think. I think I know . . .
Dad, who was on the phone? You seemed to be having an argument. *(Beat.)* Well, yeah, I did hear some of it. It was an accident. I was just here and you were talking. This is my house, too, you know. But I don't understand why. I thought you . . . You're married to Carol now. I thought that was because you and Mom . . . I don't know . . .

I know I don't seem to like Carol and I kind of don't, but . . . I'm trying to get used to it. I am getting used to it. Living with her. And I thought you kind of loved her. I mean, why else did you marry her? Am I going to have to move again? How many moms am I going to have, Dad? I just don't get it and I think it's not fair.

I kind of think it *is* my business, Dad. I have to live with these people. Am I just supposed to walk around Carol all the time now and pretend nothing's wrong? You're making me lie for you, Dad, and I'm getting sick of it. Make up your mind for once. This is crazy and really messed up. You're . . . You're being a selfish jerk. I'm really trying to still like you, Dad, but you're making it really hard.

JUST A LITTLE

Matt, comic
At home, talking to his stepmother.

It's a tattoo, Carol. Ever heard of them? *(Beat.)* You know, you're not my mother. You can't really tell me what to do, or what *not* to do. Only my real mother can do that. I don't even think my dad likes you anymore. Probably because you're so bossy.

Carol? Oh, man, this isn't right. Could you . . . not do that? You're doing much better at being a mom. Really. But you're not supposed to cry. I know that much. No matter what, you're not supposed to cry.

Well, I didn't actually mean that stuff I said. Honest. It's just that . . . well, I already have the tattoo. So there's not much you can do. Plus, you're a little bossy. I hate to say it. But could you be just a little less that way? A little? 'Cause otherwise you're . . . cool.

Calm down. I only meant like a little tiny molecular bit cool, so don't get *too* excited.

WEINER

Matt, comic
At school, talking to his teacher.

Mr. Weiner, did you ever consider changing your name? Weiner, I mean? Because I would. It's just asking for it. You may as well be named Mr. Complete Idiot or Mr. Whacked-in-the-Head or something. I'm just saying. I was thinking about it. Kids don't have to work at all to come up with an insulting nickname. It's built-in. That's not cool. I mean, once a kid called me Matt Diapers and it doesn't even make sense. It's not even close to Matt Sanders. So I couldn't really take it as an insult because he was so dumb. But you . . . Man, I don't know how you stand it. I don't know how you're alive! School must have been hell. Unless you were cool and, no offense, I don't think you were. Were you? *(Beat.)* I didn't think so.

So, how come? How come you never changed it? Especially when you decided to be a teacher. Didn't you know it was just going to start up again, going back to school? 'Cause if you worked in a bank, I bet adults would try to pretend that they didn't notice your name was Weiner. They would pretend you had a normal name that didn't mean anything else. But kids, you know they can't help themselves. So what's the deal?

DECISIONS, DECISIONS

Matt, comic
At home, talking to a friend.

I totally, absolutely, one hundred percent can't think of what to write. I hate these assignments. I didn't do anything for summer vacation and I don't know what career I want as an adult. Who cares? I'm a kid. It's not like someone's going to say, "OK, Matt, let's just blast you into space then!" Not that I want to be an astronaut. The space part sounds good, but the rest sounds boring. Science classes and all that. And I bet zero gravity gets old quick. I bet you wake up in the morning, go to brush your teeth and it's like, "Oh, crap, my toothbrush is floating over at the other end of the ship." And it's first thing in the morning and the last thing you want to do is work your way to the other end of the ship. You just woke up, for Chrissake. And for all you know, while you were sleeping the toothbrush could have floated into the toilet or something.

And don't get me started on being a banker. That's torture. All that money and you can't have it. I've heard that those bank people don't make that much. It's a wonder more of them don't get arrested. If you put me in a big vault with money, man, I'd be stealing it right, left, and center.

Is there such a job as mattress tester? I'd like that. I can do sleeping.

INTERESTING

Matt, comic
At school, talking to a friend.

Oh, man. *(Beat.)* Oh, nothing. It's just that . . . Man, these shoes hurt. That's a girl thing, I know, but man oh man . . . I thought these shoes were cool at the store, but I can tell I'm getting huge blisters. Monster-sized. It's killing me. *(Beat.)* I do not look constipated! What is that anyway? My dad always says that kind of thing, but I don't know what it means. And it's not like I'm going to look it up. Don't you hate it when people say dumb crap like, "Look it up!" Um, no. I don't actually care, so, no.

Gross! There's a condition where you can't take a crap? That sounds like a good thing. *(Beat.)* So, what happens? Do you blow up internally at some point? Or externally—God, that would be . . . Do I even need to say it!

Man, you learn something every day. Now that is interesting.

POINT

Matt, comic
At home, talking to his sister.

Mar, will you shut up? You talk too much. You can tell Dad or whoever you want, they'll all agree with me. *(Beat.)* I don't talk too much. You're full of it. That's actually funny. Me, talking too much. In case you haven't noticed, I'm a *guy*. We don't talk too much. Ever. We talk when it's necessary, unlike girls who just go on and on and on and on and on for no reason. Like right now. I am try to make a point. You are annoying. You are. And that's not just because you're my sister. It's because you obsess about you hair and stuff like that. That stuff doesn't matter. Especially when you look like a she-beast, like you do.

Don't get mad! I'm just telling you the truth. I'm just saying what other people are afraid to tell you, Marnie. You should thank me. *(Beat.)* Hey! Don't interrupt! I'm talking here. Haven't you had enough talking time for, like, the rest of time? I think so.

Again with the *me* talking too much? That's so untrue, it's funny.

THOUGHTS

Matt, comic
At school, talking to a friend.

What's so great about sunsets and puppies and all that? Who decided this stuff? How come we don't eat cats and have cobras as pets? OK, I get that one, but you know what I mean. The Indians, not the American ones, won't eat cows, right? And that's what I eat, like, all the time. Who decided this stuff? Who's in charge? And don't say God because why would the Indians not eat cows then because we're on the same planet and all. Assuming the big man in the sky exists, too. Who thought of that? That's wacky. And the idea that aliens look like little green men with big eyes. Why would they have arms and legs? Wouldn't they look completely weird, like a different form altogether? Something we can't even imagine with our puny brains? Wouldn't it be funny if space dudes were way stupider than us instead of smarter? Why do we always assume they'll be smarter? I guess 'cause they actually got here from a galaxy far, far away. But how stupid would they be to, say, come here for vacation? We're boring. I'm boring. I spend ninety percent of my life bored out of my mind.

What do you mean, you noticed? What is that supposed to mean?

LASH PARKER

Suspicious and ready for a fight, Lash has had
to take care of himself his entire life. He has
a mostly absent mother and does not know his
father.

INFINITY

Lash, dramatic
Outside, talking to a friend.

It's weird. I'm not squeamish, you know that. I can watch any movie and be totally fine. I can watch those surgery shows on TV. I'm cool with all that. But this kind of creeped me out. I never really thought about dying. I mean, I did, I have, but not as a real thing. And there that guy was. He was just . . . his skin was rotting and he didn't have a shirt on. There were bugs on him. And half of his face was gone. I mean, if you're going to shoot somebody or yourself or whatever, why would you do it in the face? And I just never thought skin could look like that.

I wasn't scared. And I didn't get sick. But it got me to thinking. I don't want to be dead. I know that sounds stupid, everyone's going to die. But I really, really don't want to. I don't want to be naked on a metal slab in the hospital. I don't even want to be old and have trouble walking to the bus stop or talking or breathing. I don't want to be old or dead. I don't know what you do about that, but I've just never wanted anything so much, I swear. I want to be like this forever. If there was a vampire right here who could promise me I could be young and alive forever, I'd be, like, "Hey, man, suck my blood. I'm begging ya." I'm serious. That was sick, seeing that dead guy. Death sucks, man.

HELPFUL

Lash, dramatic
Outside, talking to an elderly woman.

Lady? You need some help? Listen, you don't have to freak out or anything. I'm asking if I can *help*, I'm not robbing you. If I wanted to steal your purse, believe me, I could. I'm stronger than you. *(Beat.)* I said *if*. *If* I wanted to. And I don't want to. You just looked like you were having a hard time with your groceries. *(Beat.)* Just because I'm a kid and I don't look all clean-cut and nerdy doesn't mean I'm a killer or a rapist or something. No offense, but you're an old lady. I'm not really interested in you in any way; I just thought I could maybe do something good for once.

Fine, fine. I'll leave you alone. God. And people wonder why kids get violent. It's because everyone expects it. You want it. Then you can say, "I was right." I just hope you can sleep at night. Not because I'm going to come and get you, I don't give a crap about you, lady. But because you are a narrow-minded, nasty old lady. Is it so hard to believe I'm not evil? You piss me off, lady. Good luck with those groceries. Thanks to you, I'm never doing anything nice for anyone ever again.

IN THE LINE

Lash, dramatic
Outside, talking to a friend.

Don't look. Don't! Something is going down. Right now. Over there. Don't look! Man, do you have a death wish? I don't know what's going on.

Oh man! Let's get out of here. Now. *(Beat.)* What's wrong with you? Man? What the hell! Were you—are you—shot? Oh my God. Oh my God. No, man, you're fine. Let's go. Come on, I wouldn't say it if it wasn't important. We have to go, now! *(Beat.)* I know you're bleeding. It's obvious. I promise we'll take care of it, but not now. We have to go now, man. Come on; I'll help you.

What's wrong with you? Oh my God, where is everybody? Help, someone! Come on, please help! My friend is shot! Shit, won't anyone help? Stay with me, man. You'll be OK. I promise. We just have to go now.

BELIEF

Lash, dramatic
Outside, talking to a friend.

Listen, Mom, I can't be the father of anyone's baby. No way.
(Beat.) Because I'm a kid. And I didn't do anything. She just
wants me so she's trying to pin this on me. *(Beat.)* Don't yell!
You're not making any sense. You won't have to pay for my
babies. I'm smarter than that, Mom. Why are you listening to
what some girl on the street tells you? She's just trying to get
to me.

I don't know why she says that. Why do girls do anything? They
make no freakin' sense. It beats me. She's, like, obsessed with
me or something. All I know is I didn't father a baby. I don't
even like her.

I think I would know if I did, Mom. Don't you trust me at all?
God, if you don't believe what I say, who will? I almost wish I
was a father of some kid because then maybe someone would
listen to me in this world, because you don't.

LIE

Lash, dramatic
Outside, talking to a friend.

You did not see my mom at some club. First of all, no one would let you in a club. *(Beat.)* Your cousin saw her. Right. Like your cousin can tell his right hand from his left. He's high most of the time. You're both liars.

A picture. He has a picture. Naw, naw, man, my mother would not pose for pictures at a strip club. You got the wrong lady. You've seen my mom. She's, like, a mom. And she's not that stupid.

Shut up! Don't be a pervert, man! What's wrong with you? You've been hanging out with your cousin too much. You've lost it. My mom is not some . . . She was not drunk and she was not stripping. Listen, get away from me. Get out of my face. I never want to see your face again.

If I hear you saying anything else about my mom, I swear, I'll kill you.

ENJOY THE SILENCE

Lash, dramatic
At school, talking to a guidance counselor.

I don't have anything to say. *(Beat.)* Why is that so wrong? I like being quiet. Why does everyone think people are supposed to just walk around blabbering about how they feel and crap like that? Who cares? No one cares how I feel. *(Beat.)* Don't read stuff into it. I don't care how anyone else feels either. I mean, I do, but I don't. *(Beat.)* Don't you understand anything? I mean that I care about important things, but otherwise I mind my own business. Live and let live. If I'm all broken up here, boo-hoo, are you going to walk around crying all day about the sad little boy in school? I don't think so. It's all fake. You don't really care what I think, so why bother saying it? So why don't we just shut up.

Can we make a deal here? If I ever actually have something I absolutely must get off my chest, I'll find you, OK? I'll get your guidance or whatever. Otherwise, let's not bother. I'll work out my own problems. Talking *doesn't* help. Whoever came up with that idea anyway?

TAKE

Lash, dramatic
Outside, talking to a friend.

Do it. Do it! Listen, the longer you stand here thinking about it, the more likely you are to get caught. So do it, man!

Everyone steals. It's a fact of life and people who say they don't are lying. People steal cable and candy from the store and don't return library books and don't repay their friends—everyone in this whole world is a thief.

In this case, too, it's justified. That guy has been a jerk to us for years. We've come to this store a million times and never done anything wrong and he yells at us and watches us like a hawk. He already thinks we've stolen stuff we haven't, so . . . Don't be a chicken. Take it and let's get out of here. Don't be a little girl. Take it and run!

THE WINNER

Lash, semicomic
At school, talking to a teacher.

Um, Mrs. Randolph? Could I talk to you for a sec? It's just that . . . I don't want my essay read in front of the school. I know you think it's good and I appreciate that, but . . . it would make me seem . . . Do you know what I'm saying? It would just be . . . People don't think I can do school stuff. They don't know I get decent grades sometimes and I think it's better that way. They know me as . . . kinda . . . not articulate. You know, not expressing myself really good. I mean well. See, they wouldn't want to know that I could correct myself like that. You have to speak poorly—I mean bad—to get through. You know what I mean?

Is this making any sense to you? I know that you think it's gonna help to . . . I don't know . . . encourage me or something. But the thing is, Mrs. Randall, it's not. I mean, yes, but no. I'd just really like it if we kept this between us if that's OK.

AMAZING

Lash, comic
At home, talking to a friend.

I saw this show the other day on Discovery Channel about people who get these pins in their legs to make them taller. They get these pins and every day they twist this thing to pull their bones further apart. And then, eventually, new bones grow in the space they made. It's for, like, dwarves and there are people in China or something who do it.

Man, I would love to do that! I would love to grow to, like, basketball-player size! Can you imagine? You're so tall that no one gives you any crap and you could get an NBA contract for billions of dollars.

What would you do with that kind of money? *I* would get me a nice rock-star honey. You know what I'm saying? She would be fine. And maybe I'd even get a few other ladies as well—at the same time! How come just because you're tall you get all these advantages? If you're tall, it's not like basketball is a challenge. If little guys, like even midgets, did basketball, that would be exciting to watch. 'Cause if they made a slam dunk, man, that would be amazing.

OK, maybe not. Never mind.

THE ULTIMATE

Lash, comic
At home, talking to a friend.

Things must have sucked in the days before writing. Can you imagine having to keep an entire story in your head? When my mom sends me out to get bread and milk and toothpaste, I swear I forget one of them every time. It makes her so mad.

It must be weird being an immigrant, too. Like not being able to understand anyone around you. I mean, we live in a place where people can understand Spanish and English, a lot of people, but what if you spoke, maybe, Japanese? You'd be screwed. You wouldn't know what to do. You'd think maybe everyone was planning to kill you. That's what I'd think. I'd be real paranoid the whole time. But the Japanese are real smart, so they'd probably figure it out.

Wouldn't it be great to be tall *and* Japanese? Isn't there a guy like that who plays basketball? I think I saw him on TV. So he's probably, like, a genius *and* rich *and* having sexy girlfriends. Man, I wish I was tall and Japanese.

GRAY VOGEL

Gray is an outsider. He feels separate from every-one else and misunderstood. He is struggling to work out who he is. Gray has a much older brother and lives with his grandparents.

BREAK

Gray, comic
At school, talking to a friend.

Hi. Hey. Long time, no see, right? I . . . how come you're hanging out with him now? I've been forced to hang with Mel lately. *(Beat.)* What is that supposed to mean? You're acting totally weird. Are we, like, not friends anymore? 'Cause you can just say so. I really don't care. I just thought . . .

Fine. Can I ask how come? *(Beat.)* I didn't know you were that desperate and pathetic. I really didn't. That's a shock. Popularity is . . . You know the people who are popular today will be losers next week, right? That means *you*, dummy. Next week you'll be begging to hang out with me.

Well, I guess that's your choice. I mean, if you want to be a slave to what other people think, that's your choice. But don't expect me to sit around crying or anything.

So . . . I guess that's it, then. Have a nice life.

CUT

Gray, comic
At home, talking to his grandfather.

People wear their hair like this. They do. It's not 1950 anymore. *(Beat.)* I just thought it was a good idea. It looks good. It looks better than that haircut that makes me look like I joined the army. *(Beat.)* I don't want to look like other people. And I definitely don't want to be clean-cut. I'm not like other people. I'm an individual. Besides, other people *do* grow their hair—rock stars, movie stars . . . It's not against the law. In fact, I think it is the law that I should be able to do what I want. It's called freedom and we are in America, Pops. So I think I'm allowed to have long hair, even if you don't like it.

Sure, I was a good kid before. So? Things change. Get used to it. It's the new millennium. I bet aliens take over the earth soon and the first thing they do is kill everyone with a military haircut. *(Beat.)* Don't say I didn't warn you.

LOST

Gray, dramatic
At church, talking to a priest.

You can't save me. I'm nothing. Don't bother. I just need to get out: of this body, of this town, of this life.

Do you think everything's written out somewhere? That we're fated, preordained to be a certain way, to have a certain life?

Does everyone have another person that makes them important? Even if it's a best friend, it doesn't have to be, like, a husband or a wife or something. What if someone had nothing, no one? Can you just wander around the world alone forever? Do you get nuts like a guy on a desert island? I feel alone. I don't think I'll ever have anyone. So what's the point, really? I just feel wrong. Everything feels wrong. I hate who I am. I hate what I am.

I don't even know what I am. Just wrong, just sick. I don't want to talk anymore. I don't have anything else to say. Nothing I say makes sense anyway.

SLICK

Gray, comic
At school, talking to a teacher.

Mr. Hastings, why do you shave your legs? It's a little . . .
strange. I mean, that's what the other kids say. Do you, like,
dress up like a woman or something?

Oh. Is that what you do when you're a cyclist? A cyclist is when
you ride a bike, right? So, anyway, why? I mean, what difference does it make? Are you *really* hairy? Because otherwise I
can't see that it matters.

Oh. Are you mad at me? 'Cause I wasn't the only one who
wanted to know. I was just the only one who asked, that's all.
I won't tell anyone if you don't want me to. No one listens to
me anyway. No one would believe me if I told them. But they
think you dress as a woman after school, just so you know. They
say you have a big blond wig you put on, too. Just so you know.
For your information.

Don't get mad at me. I'm just the messenger, Mr. Hastings.

HELLISH

Gray, dramatic
At school, talking to a classmate.

Frank, could you stop that? Seriously, stop doing that. You're scaring me a little. What can I do to make you stop? Why are you doing this?

Sure, sure, I guess it's nice to be praying for me, but the thing is . . . I really don't want you to. Why do you think I'm going to hell anyway? *(Beat.)* Listen, I never should have told you all that stuff I was thinking. I didn't mean it. It was dumb. I was just talking. I didn't mean it. So . . . could you stop now? People think we're both nuts when you kneel down in the hallways and start praying. It's weird, dude.

Just because I think it's weird doesn't mean I'm evil. Just lay off, man. I'm sick of you. I'd rather go to hell than spend another minute talking to you.

THEM

Gray, semicomic
At school, talking to a friend.

I was just thinking, do you think we have anything in common with those kids over there? Our lives seem completely different, but maybe they're not. Like maybe that football player there secretly wants to be a woman, or maybe Susie Sherman has the hots for Becky MacMillan. It's funny to think about. That they could have this secret, shameful life. That they're really messed up just like we are. *(Beat.)* OK, OK, like *I* am. Whatever.

Face it. We're both outcasts. Do you think we were born this way or do you think it was something about how we were brought up that makes normal people not like us? Sometimes I wonder if there was something, some one thing I did wrong to make it come out this way. If I did something different, what would it be? Would I share my toys more during play time, what? It sounds stupid, but I wonder.

I bet none of them think like this. They just probably think, "Gee whiz, it's lunch time and I'm going to eat an apple." But it's nice to think that maybe after that they think, "And then I'm going to barf it up in the bathroom." It just seems like I shouldn't be the only one who's miserable around here.

AFTER SCHOOL

Gray, dramatic
At school, talking to classmates.

Would you stop calling me that? What is your problem? You know, they say people are homophobic because they're secretly gay themselves? It's true. So maybe you're the one with the problem, not me. But listen, I'm not interested. You're not my type.

You don't have to stand up for me, Trish. I can handle this. *(Beat.)* I don't know how, I just know it doesn't help for you to do my fighting for me. This is something I have to do, even if it kills me.

OK, you big, ugly baboon. You want to hit me? You're just desperate to put your hands on me, aren't you? Like I said, if you're so freaked out, you must be scared of being one yourself. So come and get me. Come on!

WISH

Gray, dramatic
At school, talking to a friend.

Do you ever think . . . If you had to die, how would you want
to die? *(Beat.) Everyone* wants to die peacefully in their sleep,
but what if you couldn't? What if you were on death row and
they said you had to die, but you could pick how. What then?

Did you know that early on in England, poor people were hung
and rich people, like royalty, got their heads chopped off? It
was, like, an honor to get your head chopped off. Even though
back then sometimes they had to chop at your head a whole
bunch of times before you died. Can you imagine not being dead
after some guy puts an ax in your neck? So, I wouldn't choose
that way.

The more you think about it, the more you realize nothing's
quick or easy. Just like living. Sometimes I think it would be
great to be put in a coma and just sleep the rest of my life. That's
my favorite part of my day, sleeping. Dreaming. Unconscious-
ness rules. Seriously. Sometimes I wish I could just be in an accident and sleep through the rest of my life.

UNDER THE BIG TOP

Gray, comic
At school, talking to a friend.

I should join the circus. I should. I'd be the most normal, boring guy there. When I say circus, I mean the carnival type with freaks. *(Beat.)* They do, too, still exist. In Mexico and places like that. I saw one on TV. I mean, if they've got wolfboys and people putting nails in their noses, I would be the most handsome, popular guy there, right? Then again, do I want some bearded lady coming on to me?

Then *again*, maybe they'd all hate me and I'd be an outcast there, too. "I hate that kid with the normal body parts. He makes me sick." Or maybe they'd say, "He thinks he's so great since he's a regular-looking guy." No, they'd probably think, "What a weirdo. He has absolutely no talent. What is he doing here? He's not special at all." Not even the freaks would like me, Mel! My life sucks.

I am not weird! You're weird! Shut up.

CHANGE

Gray, dramatic
At school, talking to a teacher.

I know I didn't do well on my test, but . . . There's just some stuff people aren't good at. This is that thing for me. I don't get it. I try. I do. But I don't get it.

I really don't know why you're bothering, Mr. Schwartz. I'm just a dumb kid. It doesn't get better than this. I swear I'm not some secret genius. Can I go now?

I could get tutoring, but . . . I really wouldn't enjoy it. What if I just tried harder?

Getting kicked out of school wouldn't be so bad. School is not a good place, Mr. Schwartz. It would actually be a big favor if you could fail me, in a way. I mean, my grandma would be mad at me, but she'd get over it. In fact, if you could get me kicked out, I'd really appreciate it, Mr. Schwartz. Would you really do that for me?

J MACKETT

J makes things look easy. Everything seems to fall into place for him. J is athletic and a natural leader. Sometimes this goes to his head. J lives with his mother and his younger sister.

GIRL STUFF

J, comic
In a store, talking to his mother.

Mom, are we done yet? This is completely embarrassing. Whatever you want to buy, just go ahead. Can I meet you somewhere else? I'm not gonna get stolen by gypsies or anything. *(Beat.)* Please, Mom. Please. Mom. Pleeeease.

You don't understand. This is *that* bad. We are in the lingerie department. I am surrounded by *(Whispering.)* bras and panties! And . . . and . . . breasts! It's not right! It's not healthy for a guy my age. Plus, it's humiliating. *(Beat.)* It's not just clothing. Because . . . Could this be any more embarrassing? Because it makes you think about stuff. It's meant to make you think about . . . women's stuff. And . . . you're my mom! I don't want to think about stuff around you. And if one of my friends saw me, I'd die.

Oh, my God. That's a girl from my class, Mom! See? Now I have to think about her wearing a . . . See, Mom? Now, please can I go? I'll just wait outside the store. Please!

SO DREAMING

J, comic
At school, talking to his friend.

Kate is a ten on the boob meter. Shelly is, like, a negative one. I've seen so many boobs it's almost boring. Not! Besides the girls in school, there's cable, the Internet, my dad's porn collection that he hides in the basement . . . Seriously. I've seen it all, man. You've got to get in the game. There are lots of girls at school who might, you know, do it with you. Maybe.

No, not Patty. She's OK, but she's a huge slut and will do it with anyone. *(Beat.)* Yeah, we did it once. It was hot.

Patty! You don't—I didn't—Don't—Stop yelling already! Come on, Steve, lets get out of here.

She's in total denial. It's sad. We did totally do it. Don't believe her. She's completely hot for me. It was so good she's probably just in shock. What a psycho!

MOMENT OF TRUTH

J, comic
At home, talking to a girl.

Do you want a drink? Do you want to watch TV? No? What do you want to do? We could play video games. Or, I don't know, go somewhere.

No, no, being alone is totally cool. Just the two of us. Me and you. Here. Alone.

No, no! I'm not nervous! I'm . . . excited. *(Beat.)* So, you sure you don't want anything? *(Beat.)* I mean, I don't want to scare you by moving too fast or anything. *(Beat.)* You're not scared? That's cool. That's cool.

Umm, maybe this is a bad idea. I mean, I don't want to interrupt your gum chewing, and my mom . . . I gotta go. Sorry. *(Beat.)* Yeah, I *know* it's my house, but . . . I gotta go now. OK? Can't I leave my own house if I want? Jeez.

THE SKINNY

J, comic
At home, talking to his mother.

Mom, this diet is cool. Much better than the last one. Have you lost a lot of weight, too? *(Beat.)* Why not? Are you cheating? *(Beat.)* You don't have to snap at me. I just asked a question. I just thought since Dad and I have lost weight that maybe . . . Are you sure you're not cheating? Because this is really easy. I've even been cheating when I'm at school, and I'm still losing weight. *(Beat.)* Huh. Well, maybe you should eat less, Mom. You ate a lot of broccoli yesterday.

You're really acting nuts, Mom. You really need to cool down. I can't help it if I have a great metabolism and you don't. In fact, I don't even think it's fair that I have to eat healthy stuff. *I'm* not overweight. Maybe you should just be happy with your body. Lots of women your age are chubby. So what?

Yeesh, what are you getting so mad about? I liked you better when you were fat.

THE BACHELOR

J, comic
At school, talking to his best friend.

I am never going to get married. Seriously, what's in it for us? *(Beat.)* Yeah, OK. I guess a wife could do your laundry. That would be good. But I can hire a maid or something. *(Beat.)* My mom will cook for me. Or I'll just eat out all the time and that's what I want to do anyway.

I just don't see that women really have a purpose as wives. I can see why they'd want husbands, since men make more money and then they can have babies. But for us, man, I don't see it. My dad always says how women are nuts. He's right. They don't make any sense. Seriously. If I'm bachelor, I can eat what I want, I don't have to pick up after myself or take showers after running. I can watch TV all night. You can't do that with women around. And who wants kids? They're a pain. Sometimes I even feel sorry for my parents, being married and having a kid like me. Just think—diapers! Gross. What if you got a really bad kid? I'm not so bad. But some kids are losers and really gassy. Man, the best thing to do is to stay single. Mark my words.

LOOK OUT

J, comic
At school, talking to his friends.

Watch, will you! Just stand outside and if he comes, let us know, Pete. Is that so hard?

Now I'm going to put the clock ahead. How far ahead do you think it should be? *(Beat.)* Ten minutes? Are you joking? It has to be more than that. *Much* more. This is Social Studies we're talking about. *(Beat.)* Come on. He's so old he doesn't even know the difference between us knocking on our desks and someone coming to the classroom door. Remember the time Pat made that ringing sound and he went looking for a phone? This guy is far gone. We could put the clock ahead forty minutes and he wouldn't know. Then someone just has to make a sound like the bell and we're home free. Simple! So stop being chicken already.

Why is everyone staring at me? Pete! Get back outside! Didn't I tell you to stand lookout? *(Beat.)* So? Is he coming? *(Beat.)* What do you mean, "He's here"? Like where "here"?

Here here. Behind me. You stink, Pete. You really stink.

BURN

J, comic
At home, talking to his mother.

Mom? Mom, it hurts. *(Beat.)* Don't be like that, Mom. Be sympathetic. Be nice. Mom, I'm hurt. I got a sunburn on my back from playing baseball. I wasn't wearing a shirt. *(Beat.)* It was hot, and there were girls around, that's why. Do we have anything for it? It burns. Seriously, it's killing me. Do you think I could have gotten cancer? 'Cause the feeling of my shirt against my skin is almost more than I can take! I'm going to have to sleep on my stomach. Is there a cure? Could I get my burned skin peeled off by a doctor or something?

I hate sunscreen, Mom. And how am I supposed to put it on my back? Besides, I didn't plan this. I hate how people tell you to be careful *after* you get hurt. You do that all the time, Mom. You know that?

How long is it going to take for this to get better? It hurts so much, Mom! How come you can't be a nurse or something good like that? It would help at times like this. There should be classes you should have to take before having a kid.

How come you're always mad at me?

HELPING

J, comic
At home, talking to his mother.

You want me to help you? Are you that old, Mom? Come on, this is embarrassing. You're . . . You're . . . I can't even look at you, Mom. You're a mess. Could you . . . fix your skirt? Have some dignity and maybe I'll help you.

Don't yell! You're drawing attention to us! How did you fall anyway? That was really uncoordinated. Sometimes I can't believe I'm your kid. I don't suppose you adopted me? 'Cause I never would have fallen into a muddy ditch. You could tell me if I'm adopted. I would understand.

I know I have your eyes. But still . . . maybe I'm Aunt Jamie's kid or something. Since she plays tennis, at least. I think maybe you should try to get up yourself, Mom. I'm worried about you. You don't exercise enough. I don't want you to die or anything.

See? I knew you could do it. Could you maybe keep your distance now so people don't know we're related? *(Beat.)* What do you mean I'm grounded? Women!

TERMS

J, comic
At school, talking to his friends.

You want me to what? Hit my head on that metal pipe ten times? Fine. That's so easy. *(Beat.)* Of course I can do it really hard. That's the whole point, isn't it? It's not a dare otherwise. I've got a really hard head. Just ask my mom. It's no problem.

But listen, first, what am I going to get if I do it? Because the satisfaction from just doing it isn't going to cut it this time. I got no satisfaction at all last time when I unhooked Gina's bra in math class and she punched me in the face. I want money. Or something good. Like your skateboard.

You've got to give if you want to get in this world. I never knew what my dad meant by that until this very minute. Pay up or shut up, guys.

KEEP YOUR DAY JOB

J, comic
At home, talking to his mother.

Can I quit school? It's really getting to be a drag. I don't think they actually teach anything. The state of our educational system is real bad. It's completely boring. Isn't there a law against that? I think it's maybe the fourteenth law. *(Beat.)* I don't know what it says. I just think it's something about an education. And you can't learn if you're falling asleep all the time. I don't know anything more than I knew when I was eight. I know the rules of football now, but that's it. The rest is junk. No one cares about facts and stuff in the world. It's not going to come up in a job.

I want to be a bodyguard or a spy. You don't need school for that. In fact, I'd be better off playing video games at home. You learn to have better reflexes and they're very educational. And I'd go to the gym, of course. So what do you say?

BILL TARTAGLIA

Bill comes from a large, close family. His house is a source of constant activity. Bill has a bad temper that flares suddenly. He lives with his parents, siblings, and grandmother.

WHAT'S IN A NAME

Bill, comic
At home, talking to his parents.

I'm not a kid anymore. Would you mind not calling me Billy? I'm Bill. That's what my friends call me. *(Beat.)* I'm not "your little Billy," Mom. You're embarrassing me in front of my friends when you say things like that. It's humiliating. Can't you sort of treat me like an adult? I'm not that far from being one. *(Beat.)* Being an adult is not about age, Dad. It's about how you feel. And I feel like Bill now. Is that too much to ask? Is this going to kill you or something? *(Beat.)* Mom, don't cry. I swear, no one else's mother acts like this. You're too . . . *(Beat.)* I'm not criticizing you. I'm just saying . . . I just want to be called Bill. That's what I'm saying. It is my name, after all. I'm still the same kid.

Yes, I'm a kid, but I'm not a kid, if you know what I mean. I'm getting too old for the clothes you buy me and getting my cheeks pinched and being called Billy. It's baby stuff and I'm sick of it!

Aw, Mom, you're such a dope. Fine, whatever. Call me Billy until I'm forty. Whatever.

IT'S RAINING, IT'S BORING

Bill, comic
At home, talking to his father.

Can we go to a movie or something? Please? I don't care which one even. I'd just really like to get out of this house. I'm bored. *(Beat.)* I can't talk to my brothers and sisters. That would be boring, too. Plus, I don't like them. *(Beat.)* Fine, fine. I do like them. Just not enough to talk to them *all day. (Beat.)* Talk to Grandma? Are you joking? *(Beat.)* Yeah, I'm sure she has a lot of interesting stories, but . . . I can't explain it. I don't want to hear any now. Why can't we get a Game Boy? *(Beat.)* Then can we go to the movies? *(Beat.)* Come on, Dad. There's not even anything on TV. And I can't go outside because it's raining. I'm trapped in the house with my *family* and I think I'm going to go nuts. Postal.

I don't want to do my homework. This family is hell. This is a literal hell on earth to be trapped in here. If anyone is looking for me, I'll be in my room dying of boredom, OK, Dad?

ALLERGIES

Bill, comic
At home, talking on the phone to a friend.

Um, I can't come over again. See, I have allergies. *(Beat.)* Your mom smokes and you have cats. I'm allergic to those things. *(Beat.)* Well, cats make my eyes water and I sneeze. And smoke, well, it just makes me feel like I'm gonna puke. *(Beat.)* It's not a wussy thing; it's a genuine condition. Medical. *(Beat.)* No, I'm not gonna die, but . . . who wants to be sick?

Can't we just go to my house instead? I know there are way too many people there, but— *(Beat.)* You can't be allergic to my grandma. It doesn't work like that. No way a doctor told you that. Believe me, I know there are too many girls at my house. I know that so well, but maybe just this once . . . until I can see an allergist or something? Look I'm sorry, but also my mom actually says there's no way I can come to your house.

I am not whipped! You're whipped!

DESTROYED

Bill, comic
At home, talking to his father and sister.

You didn't! Lucy! You broke my robot! Stupid kid! *(Beat.)* Mom, Dad, Lucy broke my robot! Stupid little baby. I can't believe you. I hate this house! I am going to fail science now, you stupid, little moron.

Why are you yelling at me, Dad? I didn't break anything. Stupid Lucy did. Why does she have to touch my things? I told her not to! I am going to fail out of school now.

I shouldn't have left it out? Where should I have left it? Is there any place in this entire universe that's mine where I can leave my stuff? No! I have no privacy. And she should have kept her hands to herself. How can you blame *me* for what she did? This is typical! I'm always wrong.

Well, fine. I'm going to my room with my broken robot that took *four weeks* to make. I guess now instead of going to regular college, I'll go to clown college because I *failed out of school*. Thanks a lot, stupid family. I hate you!

GENETICS

Bill, comic
At school, talking to a teacher and a friend.

Can I ask a question about genes, Ms. Barker? How much do they really determine? I mean, am I going to go bald because all the other guys in my family did? Please say no.

Oh, man, Gerry. I don't want to be bald. My dad was saying the other day that he lost his hair when he was young. Who knows how many days I have left? How young can someone lose their hair, do you think? I know you can lose it really early, anytime, if you have cancer. But if you don't? Do you think my dad had . . . Oh, God, I hope not. Do you think I'm dying, Gerry? *(Beat.)* No, no. That is stupid. I would know, right? And I feel fine except for this losing my hair thing.

I don't want to be one of those guys in the "I Have Fake Hair and Now I Can Go Swimming" commercials. I don't want to be eighteen with a big, shiny head! What should I do? *(Beat.)* I know it's years from now, but I have to mentally prepare myself! Think about it. I have to get a girl to marry me before my hair falls out and right now I can't get one to puke on me!

DOOMED

Bill, comic
At school, talking to his classmates.

I wish my mom didn't make me be in band. I wouldn't mind so much if I got to play a sexy instrument. You know what I mean. Like one you could play as a rock star, too. Drums or something. But clarinet? Hopeless. Nothing my parents make me do prepares me for life. They just don't get it. No one high fives you in the hallway when you make first chair. No one cares. It's not ever going to make us liked or cool. Sometimes you see supermodels with these ugly guys. How did they do it? They have money. I don't think there's ever been a rich clarinet player. It's a sick system.

Hey, Melanie, can I ask you a question? Would you like a guy only for his money? And, if so, would that make you like a prostitute?

Girls are so sensitive! How hard is it to make a billion dollars? 'Cause I think I need all the help I can get!

BRAINS VERSUS BRAUN

Bill, comic
At school, talking to a friend.

How wussy would it be if I pretended to be sick? *(Beat.)* Did you hear him? We're playing *dodgeball* today. Aren't we too old for that? I can already see the circle-sized bruises all over me. Dodgeball is the most brutal game on earth. And the most personal. I mean, in baseball no one brutally gangs up on one player. It's not possible. This is school-approved geek bashing. This is like—what is it called?—survival of the fittest. We both know I am not the fittest. It's my mom's fault. She never let me play sports as a kid. Always made me stay inside, helping her fold laundry.

You know, I don't even think I need to fake being sick. I feel like I'm gonna puke. *(Beat.)* I know I'm being a wimp. Maybe . . . maybe I'll just trip over the ball right at the beginning of the game and get out. That's what I'll do.

Ha! I'm a genius!

BEGGING FOR IT

Bill, comic
Outside, talking to a stranger and a friend.

I can't give it to you. *(Beat.)* Because it's not actually mine, it's my parents'. Listen, I have to go. Really. And I can't give you money, mister, it's my mom and dad's.

I'm being serious here. I *have* change, but I can't *give* it to you. It's my parent's money. What aren't you getting here? Maybe that's why you're poor. You don't listen! Plus, you'll only use the money to buy alcohol or drugs. So what's the point? It's not helping. If you used the money to buy toothpaste or something, that would be a worthwhile cause.

Back off! My dad's Italian. I'll get him to kill you if you don't back off.

Shut up, Gerry. I know my dad just sells furniture, but he doesn't!

YOUNGER MAN

Bill, comic
At school, talking to a friend.

You know what? I think I could get a girlfriend online. I could use a picture of my older brother. *(Beat.)* No, it could work! I'd email her and call her on the phone. We could drag it out for a while, I bet. And then when we finally met, she'd be so in love with me, she wouldn't care how old I was or what I looked like or anything. I mean, she's looking for a boyfriend on the net, how much could she really care?

I'd love having an older girlfriend. She'd wear high heels all the time and wouldn't be nervous, so I wouldn't have to be. She'd be . . . *experienced.* And she could buy me alcohol and cigarettes so I'd be popular at school.

I am not dreaming! It could happen! You see stories like this on the news all the time! Older women really like young men!

You know what, don't talk to me. You don't know anything.

BOY VERSUS GIRL

Bill, comic
At school, talking to a friend.

Ash, could you come up for air sometime? I've been listening to you go on and on about Brian Miller for an hour now. I don't think I can take it anymore. Why don't you ask him out? *(Beat.)* Of course you can ask him out. He'd probably be relieved. I'd love it if a girl asked me out. You have no idea the terror involved in asking someone out. It's unbelievable. In fact, I'd say that's my ideal girl. One who'd ask me out. I'm going to hold out for that one, ballsy girl. I hate the whole boy-girl thing. It's too nerve-wracking.

P.S., Ashley: It's really unpleasant to listen to how cute another guy is if you're a guy, too. What if I sat here and went on and on about every other girl in school? You wouldn't like that, would you? *(Beat.)* You wouldn't care? Oh, thanks. Thanks a lot. That's just great. You can be really cruel, Ash, you know that? Man, that hurt.

THE AUTHOR

Kristen Dabrowski is an actress, writer, acting teacher, and director. She received her MFA from The Oxford School of Drama in Oxford, England. The actor's life has taken her all over the United States and England. Her other books, published by Smith and Kraus, include *111 Monologues for Middle School Actors Volume 1*, *The Ultimate Audition Book for Teens 3*, and *20 Ten-Minute Plays for Teens Volume 1*. Currently, she lives in the world's smallest apartment in New York City. You can contact the author at monologuemadness@yahoo.com.